In the same series by Roland Fiddy:
The Fanatic's Guide to Cats
The Fanatic's Guide to Computers
The Fanatic's Guide to Dads
The Fanatic's Guide to Husbands
The Fanatic's Guide to Sex

First published in hardback in the USA in 1995 by Exley Giftbooks
Published in Great Britain in 1995 by Exley Publications Ltd.

12 11 10 9 8 7 6 5 4 3 2 1

ISBN 1-85015-635-2

Printed at Oriental Press, UAE.

Exley Publications Ltd, 16 Chalk Hill, Watford, Herts, WD1 4BN, United Kingdom.
Exley Giftbooks, 232 Madison Avenue, Suite 1206, NY 10016, USA.

Golf is not only recreational . . .

. . . it is also useful.

The fanatical golfer addressing the ball.

The fanatical golfer should not worry about his standard of play,
as this will affect his standard of play.

Nothing must interfere with his concentration.

The fanatical golfer never misses an opportunity to improve his . . .

. . . er – or her putting.

La Ronde

The fanatical golfer knows how important
it is not to rush the back swing.

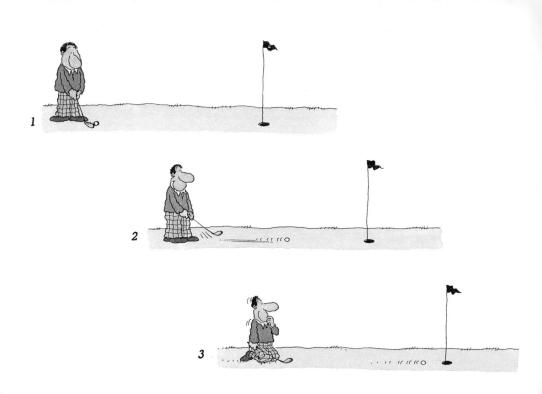

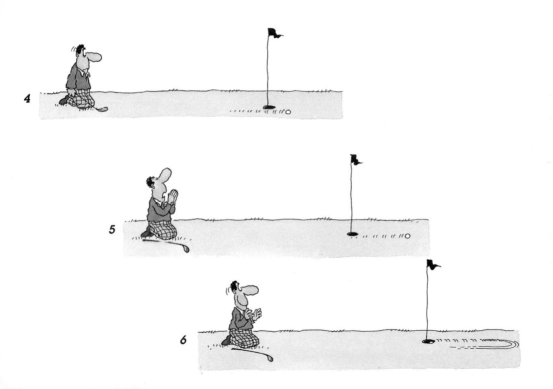

1

You must not carry more than fourteen clubs in your bag . . .

2

. . . this is a sensible rule for obvious reasons.

Play the ball as it lies.

Fanatical golfers need to be specially patient with beginners . . .

This is against the Rules . . .

. . . and so is this.

1

2

"Old men forget; yet all shall be forgot,
But he'll remember with advantages, What feats he did that day . . ."
(Shakespeare: Henry V)

The fanatical golfer finds it hard to accept criticism . . .

. . . or to ignore it . . .

The fanatical golfer understands the importance ...

. . . of controlling one's temperament.

The game is full of surprises.

The angler and the golfer swopping stories.

Golf: the ideal combination of recreation and exercise.

Books in the "Crazy World" series

($4.99 £2.99 paperback)

The Crazy World of Aerobics (Bill Stott)
The Crazy World of Cats (Bill Stott)
The Crazy World of Cricket (Bill Stott)
The Crazy World of Gardening (Bill Stott)
The Crazy World of Golf (Mike Scott)
The Crazy World of The Handyman (Roland Fiddy)
The Crazy World of Hospitals (Bill Stott)
The Crazy World of Housework (Bill Stott)
The Crazy World of Love (Roland Fiddy)
The Crazy World of Marriage (Bill Stott)
The Crazy World of The Office (Bill Stott)
The Crazy World of Photography (Bill Stott)
The Crazy World of Rugby (Bill Stott)
The Crazy World of Sailing (Peter Rigby)
The Crazy World of Sex (David Pye)
The Crazy World of Soccer (Bill Stott)

Books in the "Fanatics" series

($6.99 £3.99 hardback, also available in a larger
paperback format, $4.99 £2.99)

The **Fanatic's Guides** are perfect presents for
everyone with a hobby that has got out of hand. Over
fifty hilarious colour cartoons by Roland Fiddy.

The Fanatic's Guide to Cats
The Fanatic's Guide to Computers
The Fanatic's Guide to Dads
The Fanatic's Guide to Golf
The Fanatic's Guide to Husbands
The Fanatic's Guide to Sex

Books in the "Victim's Guide" series

($4.99 £2.99 paperback)

Award-winning cartoonist Roland Fiddy sees the
funny side to life's phobias, nightmares and
catastrophes.

The Victim's Guide to the Baby
The Victim's Guide to the Christmas
The Victim's Guide to the Dentist
The Victim's Guide to the Doctor
The Victim's Guide to Middle Age

Great Britain: Order these super books from
your local bookseller or from Exley Publications
Ltd, 16 Chalk Hill, Watford, Herts WD1 4BN.
(Please send £1.30 to cover postage and packing
on 1 book, £2.60 on 2 or more books.)